REMARKABLE PEOPLE

Oprah Winfrey

by Heather C. Hudak

Published by Weigl Publishers Inc.
350 5th Avenue, Suite 3304, PMB 6G
New York, NY 10118-0069

Website: www.weigl.com
Copyright ©2010 WEIGL PUBLISHERS INC.

All of the Internet URLs given in the book were valid at the time of publication.
However, due to the dynamic nature of the Internet, some addresses may have
changed, or sites may have ceased to exist since publication. While the author and
publisher regret any inconvenience this may cause readers, no responsibility for any
such changes can be accepted by either the author or the publisher.

Library of Congress Cataloging-in-Publication Data

Hudak, Heather C., 1975-
 Oprah Winfrey / Heather C. Hudak.
    p. cm. -- (Remarkable people)
 Includes index.
 ISBN 978-1-60596-630-4 (hard cover : alk. paper) -- ISBN 978-1-60596-631-1 (soft
cover : alk. paper)
1. Winfrey, Oprah--Juvenile literature. 2. Television personalities--United States--
Biography--Juvenile literature. 3. Actors--United States--Biography--Juvenile
literature. I. Title.
 PN1992.4.W56H84 2009
 791.4502'8092--dc22
 [B]
                              2009005630

Printed in China
1 2 3 4 5 6 7 8 9 0 13 12 11 10 09

Editor: Heather C. Hudak
Design: Terry Paulhus

Photograph Credits
Weigl acknowledges Getty Images as the primary image supplier for this title.
Unless otherwise noted, all images herein were obtained from Getty Images and
its contributors.

Every reasonable effort has been made to trace ownership and to obtain
permission to reprint copyright material. The publishers would be pleased
to have any errors or omissions brought to their attention so that they may
be corrected in subsequent printings.

Contents

Who Is Oprah Winfrey?

As one of the world's most successful **businesswomen**, Oprah Winfrey leads a company called Harpo Productions. Created in 1988, the company promotes Oprah's image as a well-known talk show host, actress, and spokesperson. In addition to Harpo Productions, Oprah owns *O, The Oprah Magazine*. She also encourages people to read and promotes authors through Oprah's Book Club. In 2008, Oprah announced that she would launch the Oprah Winfrey Network (OWN) with Discovery Communications in 2009. Shows airing on OWN will aim to help people live up to their potential. In addition to her work as a businesswoman and talk show host, Oprah uses her fame to help charities and people around the world. In 1997, Oprah started Oprah's Angel Network. This organization helps others in need. Oprah has won many awards for her work on and off screen. She has become an **inspiration** to people all over the world.

> *"The big secret in life is that there is no big secret. Whatever your goal, you can get there if you're willing to work."*

Growing Up

Oprah was born on January 29, 1954, in Kosciusko, Mississippi. Her parents, Vernita Lee and Vernon Winfrey, were not married. They were not ready to raise a child, so Oprah lived on a farm with her grandmother. Oprah and her grandmother had very little money. Oprah did not have toys or friends to play with.

In kindergarten, Oprah wrote a letter to her teacher asking to skip a grade. The next day, Oprah began grade one. Later, she skipped grade two.

Oprah moved to Milwaukee, Wisconsin, when she was six years old. Here, Oprah lived with her mother, who worked as a housecleaner.

Milwaukee is the largest city in Wisconsin.

Get to Know Mississippi

ANIMAL
White-tailed Deer

FLAG

BIRD
Mockingbird

MISSISSIPPI

| 0 | 100 Miles |
| 0 | 100 Kilometers |

Mississippi became the 20th state of the United States on December 10, 1817.

The world's largest cottonwood tree plantation is located in Mississippi.

In 1963, the medical center at the University of Mississippi completed the world's first human lung **transplant**.

In 1914, the first female rural mail carrier in the United States delivered mail by buggy in Mississippi.

Mississippi is the home of North America's rarest cranes. Sandhill cranes live in Mississippi's grassy savannas.

Think about it!

How might living in the state of Mississippi have **influenced** Oprah? Research your state's sites and symbols, and write about how they might have influenced you and your family.

Practice Makes Perfect

Oprah was a talented speaker at a very young age. By age three, She was reciting Bible verses at her grandmother's church. Oprah also enjoyed reading, It allowed her to use her imagination to escape her poor living conditions.

When Oprah was 14 years old, her mother sent her to live with her father in Nashville, Tennessee. Vernon helped Oprah earn good grades at school. Oprah's grades won her a school trip to the White House. A local radio station talked to her about the trip. They liked Oprah's voice and hired her to host a radio show. Oprah began her radio career at 16 years of age.

■ Radio hosts must speak well and be organized. They also must know how to operate studio equipment.

Oprah won a public-speaking contest in her teens. This success earned her money for a college education. Oprah practiced public speaking, worked hard, and **invested** her money wisely. Later, she studied speech and acting at Tennessee State University. Oprah also won two beauty contests. These successes helped her earn a job as a television news reporter.

QUICK FACTS

- A spelling mistake on Oprah's birth certificate changed her name from Orpah to Oprah. Orpah comes from the Book of Ruth in the Bible.
- The only women who owned production studios before Oprah were actresses Mary Pickford and Lucille Ball.
- The Harpo Productions company name is Oprah's name spelled backward.

Reading, writing, public speaking, and business sense were important to Oprah's success. Later, Oprah used stories from her troubled life to relate to her viewers. She talked about her problems, failures, and fears on television.

■ Oprah's speaking abilities won her a four-year scholarship to Tennessee State University.

At 19, Oprah became the youngest television news **anchor** and the first female African American anchor at a television station in Nashville. Soon, Oprah moved to Baltimore, Maryland. She became co-host of the morning talk show *People Are Talking*. Oprah worked on the show for eight years.

Oprah moved to Chicago in 1984. There, she hosted a talk show called *A.M. Chicago*. Soon after, Oprah played the role of Sofia in the movie *The Color Purple*. She earned an **Academy Award nomination** for her acting.

In 1986, Oprah began working on her own talk show. On *The Oprah Winfrey Show*, Oprah talked about her life. The show was a success and earned Oprah respect and wealth. With her money, she bought the show from the American Broadcasting Company (ABC) and started Harpo Productions. Oprah became the third woman in history to own a major production studio. *The Oprah Winfrey Show* earns millions of dollars each year.

■ In 2005, Oprah produced the Broadway musical based on *The Color Purple*. The live show now tours across the country.

Thoughts from Oprah

Talk shows present many different topics to viewers. They often explore issues and values that society is questioning at the time. Oprah has discussed a range of subjects in her role as a talk-show host.

Oprah dreams big.

"The biggest adventure you can ever take is to live the life of your dreams."

Oprah talks about Barack Obama becoming president.

"I was so, so, so excited, and then just sort of a calm came over me. It feels like it actually is kind of real, so it feels great."

Oprah talks about overcoming obstacles as a child.

"I knew there was a way out. I knew there was another kind of life because I had read about it. I knew there were other places, and there was another way of being."

Oprah is not afraid of failure.

"Think like a queen. A queen is not afraid to fail. Failure is another stepping stone to greatness."

Oprah talks about launching the Oprah Winfrey Network.

"I'll now have the opportunity to do this 24 hours a day on a platform that goes on forever."

Oprah talks about being successful.

"Unless you choose to do great things with it, it makes no difference how much you are rewarded, or how much power you have."

What Is a Talk Show Host?

A talk show host asks well-known or interesting people to answer questions on TV or radio shows. There is no **script** for the show, though the questions are usually written ahead of time. Guests answer the questions and talk about their lives.

Producing a talk show is not easy. Many people work together to create each show. First, there must be an idea for the show. Next, someone must contact guests to appear on the show.

The lighting crew aims bright lights at the host and guests. A sound crew makes sure the host and guests have microphones. The camera crew films the show. These are just a few of the people who help produce each show.

■ Many people work behind the scenes to produce a talk show.

Talk Show Hosts 101

Larry King (1933–)

In 1957, Larry King began his career as a radio show host in Florida. Three years later, he took a job hosting a TV show called *Miami Undercover*. In the 70s, Larry worked as a sports broadcaster and on other radio talk shows. Larry is best known for hosting the *Larry King Live Show*, which first aired on CNN in 1985. To date, Larry has interviewed more than 40,000 people and has received many awards for his work, including the Peabody Award for Excellence in broadcasting for both radio and TV.

Ellen Degeneres (1958–)

Ellen Degeneres is an entertainment talk show host. Ellen began her career as a comedian in the 1980s. In the mid-1990s and early 2000s, Ellen starred in two TV comdies, *Ellen* and *The Ellen Show*. In 2003, she began hosting a daytime TV talk show. She has won many Daytime **Emmy Awards** for her work on this show.

Rachael Ray (1968–)

Rachael Ray is a cook who has hosted many TV shows, including *30 Minute Meals*, *Rachael Ray's Tasty Travels*, *$40 a Day*, and *Inside Dish*. She also has authored a number of best-selling cookbooks and launched a magazine called *Every Day with Rachael Ray*. In 2005, Rachael signed a deal with Oprah Winfrey to host a daytime talk show. The show first aired in 2006.

Barbara Walters (1929–)

Barbara Walters is a news and entertainment talk show host. Barbara began writing for *The Today Show* on NBC in 1961. Over the next year, she worked her way up to handling story assignments, interviews, and reporting. In 1974, Barbara became the first female host of *The Today Show*. Later, she became co-host of the *ABC Evening News* and a regular on *20/20*. Barbara has hosted many interview shows and is also a co-host on the daytime talk show *The View*.

Microphone

A microphone is a tool people use to record their voices or make them louder. They are used when people perform live or so that they can be heard on television and radio. Alexander Graham Bell made the first microphone in 1876 when he invented the telephone. This microphone was used to **transmit** voices.

Influences

Oprah's grandmother had a strong influence on Oprah as a child. Her grandmother encouraged her to read and work hard. Many times, Oprah heard her grandmother refer to her as a "gifted" child. Though Oprah did not know what this meant at the time, it made her feel special.

Later, Oprah lived with her father, Vernon. He also played a big role in her life. Vernon was very strict. He had many rules that Oprah had to follow. These included preparing a book report each week, getting good grades in school, and coming home by curfew. Vernon wanted Oprah to live the best life possible. He helped her achieve her goals through hard work and strict discipline.

■ Vernon Winfrey had a strong influence on Oprah.

Oprah has said that author Maya Angelou is her mentor. After reading Maya's *I Know Why the Caged Bird Sings*, Oprah felt an instant bond with the author. They shared many similar life experiences as young girls growing up in the southern United States. Oprah met Maya more than 20 years ago, and they have been friends ever since.

STEDMAN GRAHAM

Stedman Graham is a best-selling author, businessman, and entrepreneur. He heads a management and marketing company called S. Graham & Associates. Through this company, Stedman travels the United States giving speeches and hosting workshops. Stedman is also the founder of AAD, a nonprofit organization that helps children in need learn leadership skills.

■ Oprah has been in a relationship with Stedman Graham since 1986.

Overcoming Obstacles

As a child, Oprah was **abused**. Reading books made Oprah feel better. She put her troubles aside and focused on school. Oprah believed she could become a successful person.

Oprah attended college in the 1970s. At this time, few African Americans went to college. African Americans were not always given the opportunities that other people had. Television stations worried that people would not watch an African American anchor. Viewers enjoyed watching Oprah. She was honest and open about her feelings. This helped Oprah become a successful talk show host.

■ Oprah has been very open about her weight problems. She connects with many people because of her openness.

In the 1990s, many talk shows featured topics that shocked audiences and created conflict. These shows were very popular. Oprah did not want her show to become **sensationalist**. The ratings for *The Oprah Winfrey Show* dropped. Over time, people began to appreciate Oprah's approach.

Over the years, Oprah has struggled to lose weight. **Dieticians**, diet experts, and gym trainers have helped Oprah learn to control her weight. She has learned to be happy with her size, as long as she is healthy. Viewers appreciate that Oprah shares their problems with weight loss and gain.

■ Oprah follows a diet and exercise program to help her control her weight and stay healthy. Trainer Bob Greene works with Oprah to help her eat right and get fit.

Achievements and Successes

More than 44 million viewers in 144 countries watch *The Oprah Winfrey Show* each week. It is the top-rated talk show in television history. Oprah and the show have won dozens of Emmy Awards.

In 1986, Oprah acted in the movie *Native Son*. She played herself in the 1987 film *Throw Momma from the Train*. Oprah acted in the 1998 movie *Beloved*. She has also appeared on television shows and movies, such as *The Women of Brewster Place*.

In 1996, Oprah began Oprah's Book Club to encourage people to read more often. Oprah selects a book she would like others to read. Then, she sets a date to talk about the book on television. The club has thousands of members worldwide. Each book featured by the club has become a bestseller.

THE OPRAH MAGAZINE

SUCCESS!
Define it for yourself

Never Say Never
Amazing women who prove you can do anything

Fall's delicious **new clothes**

What a charming guy!
OPRAH talks to TOM HANKS

OPRAH.COM

■ Oprah is the richest African American woman.

Oprah has won many important awards, including a Lifetime Achievement Award from the National Academy of Television Arts & Sciences. In 2001, *Newsweek* magazine named Oprah "Woman of the Century." Oprah was added to the National Association for the Advancement of Colored People (NAACP) Hall of Fame in 2005. *TIME* magazine has named Oprah one of the 100 most influential people in the world many times.

Many magazines print stories about Oprah. She has been featured in *Essence*, *Vogue*, *Newsweek*, *People*, and *InStyle*.

THE OPRAH WINFREY FOUNDATION

Through The Oprah Winfrey Foundation, Oprah has given millions of dollars to organizations that support education and empowerment. In 2002, the foundation provided funds to 63 South African schools to build libraries, as well as to pay for food, clothing, books, and other supplies for 50,000 South African children. Later, Oprah started The Oprah Winfrey Leadership Academy Foundation to fund the building of Oprah's Leadership Academy for Girls near Johannesburg, South Africa.

In 1998, Oprah established Oprah's Angel Network, which urges people to **donate** to those in need. The network has raised more than $80 million in donations. The money is used to help people pay for college and to build homes and schools.

Write a Biography

A person's life story can be the subject of a book. This kind of book is called a biography. Biographies describe the lives of remarkable people, such as those who have achieved great success or have done important things to help others. These people may be alive today, or they may have lived many years ago. Reading a biography can help you learn more about a remarkable person.

At school, you might be asked to write a biography. First, decide who you want to write about. You can choose a talk show host, such as Oprah Winfrey, or any other person you find interesting. Then, find out if your library has any books about this person. Learn as much as you can about him or her. Write down the key events in this person's life. What was this person's childhood like? What has he or she accomplished? What are his or her goals? What makes this person special or unusual?

A concept web is a useful research tool. Read the questions in the following concept web. Answer the questions in your notebook. Your answers will help you write your biography review.

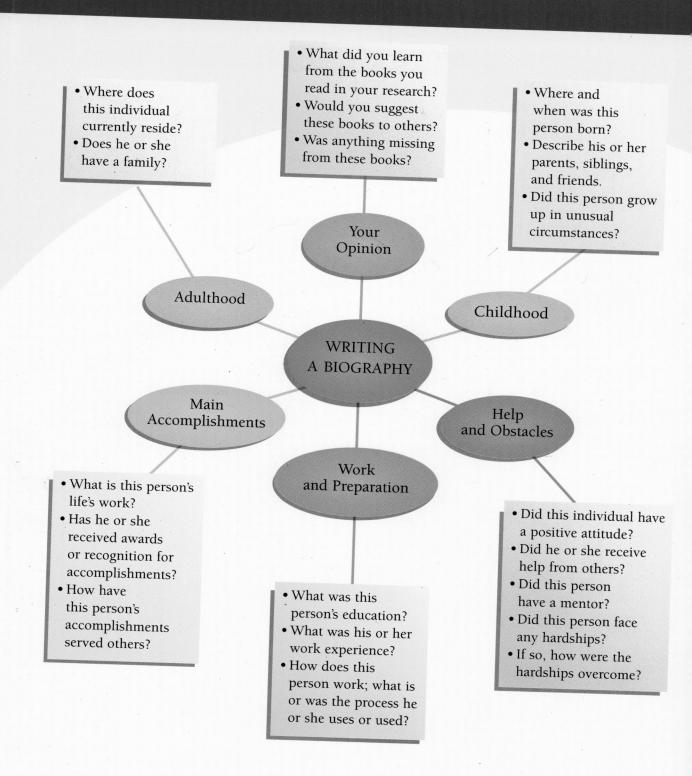

- Where does this individual currently reside?
- Does he or she have a family?

- What did you learn from the books you read in your research?
- Would you suggest these books to others?
- Was anything missing from these books?

- Where and when was this person born?
- Describe his or her parents, siblings, and friends.
- Did this person grow up in unusual circumstances?

Your Opinion

Adulthood

Childhood

WRITING A BIOGRAPHY

Main Accomplishments

Help and Obstacles

Work and Preparation

- What is this person's life's work?
- Has he or she received awards or recognition for accomplishments?
- How have this person's accomplishments served others?

- What was this person's education?
- What was his or her work experience?
- How does this person work; what is or was the process he or she uses or used?

- Did this individual have a positive attitude?
- Did he or she receive help from others?
- Did this person have a mentor?
- Did this person face any hardships?
- If so, how were the hardships overcome?

Timeline

YEAR	OPRAH WINFREY	WORLD EVENTS
1954	Oprah is born on January 29, 1954, in Kosciusko, Mississippi.	In 1954, the United States Supreme Court bans **racial segregation** in public schools.
1968	In 1968, Oprah's mother sends her to live with her father in Nashville, Tennessee.	In 1968, civil rights leader Martin Luther King Jr., is killed in Memphis, Tennessee.
1977	Oprah becomes a morning talk show host in Baltimore, Maryland, in 1977.	In 1977, fifteen countries, including the United States, sign a pact to stop producing nuclear weapons.
1986	In 1986, Oprah starts hosting a talk show called *The Oprah Winfrey Show*.	The spacecraft, *Voyager 2*, discovers new information about the planet Uranus in 1986.
1996	In 1996, Oprah begins Oprah's Book Club.	In 1996, Prince Charles and Princess Diana of Great Britain divorce after 15 years of marriage.
2005	Oprah is inducted to the National Association for the Advancement of Colored People (NAACP) Hall of Fame.	YouTube.com goes online, allowing users around the world to share videos and communicate.
2009	Oprah begins airing the Best Life Series on her talk show. The aim is to help people lead healthier, happier lives.	Barack Obama is sworn in as president of the United States.

Further Research

How can I find out more about Oprah Winfrey?

Most libraries have computers that connect to a database that contains information on books and articles about different subjects. You can input a key word and find material on the person, place, or thing you want to learn more about. The computer will provide you with a list of books in the library that contain information on the subject you searched for. Non-fiction books are arranged numerically, using their call number. Fiction books are organized alphabetically by the author's last name.

Websites

Harpo Productions, Inc.
www.oprah.com

Academy of Achievement
www.achievement.org/autodoc/page/win0bio-1

Words to Know

abused: to be hurt or injured

Academy Award nomination: being chosen to run for an acting award for movie performers and producers

anchor: a person who hosts news programs

businesswomen: women who do business or work for a company

dieticians: people who help others learn to eat healthy

donate: to give to a good cause

Emmy Awards: awards for television performers

influenced: had or exercised power

inspiration: something that moves a person to create

invested: spent money on something in the hope of making more money

racial segregation: separation by race

script: the written version of a play or a movie intended for an audience

sensationalist: doing shocking or vulgar things in order to gain attention

transmit: to send a signal from place to place

transplant: medically move an organ from one person to another person

Index